Penguin Books

Conversations with Children

R. D. Laing was born in Glasgow in 1927, and was educated at a grammar school and at Glasgow University, where he graduated as a doctor of medicine in 1951. From 1951 to 1953 he was a psychiatrist in the British Army, and then worked at the Glasgow Royal Mental Hospital in 1955; the Department of Psychological Medicine at the University of Glasgow in 1956; and the Tavistock Clinic in 1957–61. He was director of the Langham Clinic, London, 1962–5. From 1961 until 1967 he did research into families with the Tavistock Institute of Human Relations, as a Fellow of the Foundations Fund for Research in Psychiatry.

Since 1964, Dr Laing has been Chairman of the Philadelphia Association Ltd, 'a charity whose members, associates, students, and friends are concerned to develop appropriate human responses, to those of us who are under mental or emotional stress but do not want psychiatric treatment.'

As a psychoanalyst and psychiatrist, his research and therapy have focused for some years on very disturbed types of interaction in institutions, groups, and families.

His books include **The Divided Self, Self and Others, Interpersonal Perception** (with H. Phillipson and A. R. Lee), **Reason and Violence** (with D. Cooper), **Sanity, Madness and the Family** (with A. Esterson), **The Politics of Experience** and the **Bird of Paradise, Knots, The Politics of the Family, The Facts of Life**, and **Do You Love Me?** Dr Laing has also written many reviews and articles in scientific periodicals.

By the same author

The Divided Self

Self and Others

Reason and Violence

Sanity, Madness and the Family
(*with Aaron Esterson*)

Interpersonal Perception

The Politics of Experience and The Bird of Paradise

Knots

The Politics of the Family

The Facts of Life

Do You Love Me?

R. D. Laing

CONVERSATIONS
WITH CHILDREN

Penguin Books

Penguin Books Ltd, Harmondsworth,
Middlesex, England
Penguin Books, 625 Madison Avenue,
New York, New York 10022, U.S.A.
Penguin Books Australia Ltd, Ringwood,
Victoria, Australia
Penguin Books Canada Ltd, 2801 John Street,
Markham, Ontario, Canada L3R 1B4
Penguin Books (N.Z.) Ltd, 182–190 Wairau Road,
Ackland 10, New Zealand

First published 1978
Published simultaneously by Allen Lane
Reprinted 1982

Copyright © R. D. Laing, 1978
All rights reserved

Made and printed in Great Britain by
Hazell Watson & Viney Ltd, Aylesbury, Bucks
Set in Monotype Rockwell

To my family

Introduction

The conversations in this anthology were written down by me
from memory over a six-year period as part of a journal I
keep. They are all recorded from memory. No tape record
ever was used. Nearly all were committed to paper within
twenty-four hours of occurring.

None of them was structured or set up. They
are without exception part of the flux of uncontrived hap-
penings that occur in the course of my family life. The children
are in the habit of seeing me jotting things down; a lot of my
writing is done here or there, often with other people, in-
cluding children, around. I do not think that the fact of writing
them down has significantly affected their character.

I've always enjoyed dialogue, repartee, and
interplay and reciprocity generally, with and without words.
However I have spent a considerable part of my life
studying unenjoyable communication, miscommunication,
and failure to communicate, much of it in family contexts,
and in depicting, describing and theorizing about this domain
of misery. I have done so, largely because I attribute such
importance to the way we get on or not, with the people we
live with. It affects everything; our intellectual, spiritual
and physical lives, as well as our emotional and social. And
has immense consequences on how we spend our time
outside the family, 'making' history, etc.

Those who have studied painful interactions
have documented many ways in which we may do one another
in, not always knowing we are doing so, or being so done to.
Many nuances of ways we may confuse, deceive and mystify
ourselves and others, without often realizing we are, have
been described by the experts in this division of hell in
recent years.

However, the other side of the story has not been looked at nearly so much. The language of the happy dialogue of intelligent beings has evolved to an amazing degree of intricacy and complexity. When it is not knotted, entangled and entangling, then instead of this being a deadening suffocating zone, it is the free and open space between us where we can play with reality together, where we question and answer, inquire into what is the case and what is not, for the sheer heaven of it. The patterns of reciprocity which are spun out of this activity synchronously and diachronically are most succinctly epitomized for me, in music, through counterpoint, in visual terms, in the *interlace*.

It is therefore a great pleasure and relief for me to present these dialogues which express so much light-hearted and serious delight; not that they are not sometimes fierce and savage, not that the dark side of things is missing, but that, it seems to me, so far, hatred, spite, revenge, jealousy, malice and envy, and the other blights on life, are not seen here triumphant.

In the following pages, we are able to observe the emotional and cognitive development of two children with unimpaired faculties unfold within the interlace and interweave of relations with adults whom they do not fear and whom they like as they are liked.

After pondering it over a lot, I have decided not to introduce their conversations with a theoretical essay on them, nor to footnote them in the many places where I have felt tempted to do so. The best order, I think, is to let them stand on their own, and for them to be read, in the first place, with the fewest possible theoretical presuppositions. Such theoretical considerations raised by them in many relevant fields, psychoanalysis, developmental epistemology, communications theory, anthropology, can be taken up later. In the meantime, I hope the professionals will find them useful. Yes, so many constructions can be placed on them! In these pages I shall not talk across or over them with my adult voice. Since this book is almost entirely taken up with the voices of children I expect it may be read as much by children as by adults, and since it needs no professional or scientific expertise, that it will be read as readily by anyone as by adult child 'experts'.

I hope that these pages will contribute to making apparent that it is just as useful for adults to be in touch with children as it is for children to be in touch with adults. We learn about children, only from children. Our understanding of ourselves is enormously impoverished if we are out of touch with childhood. Adults can suffer as much from the deprivation of children in their lives as the other way round. I suspect that children play as important a part in adult 'growth and development' as we adults do in theirs. I don't spend time with them because I have to, or because I should, but simply because I want to.

Having studied human communication for many years professionally, I am very aware of what is left out in this book. There are very few indications of the tempo, rhythm, pitch, volume and timbre of the words on the page, and hardly anything about the movements, expressions and gestures which are inextricably part of the interactional dance.

These conversations emerge out of the time before spoken speech. Both Adam and Natasha enjoyed and enjoy, with no break of continuity, a most intimate reciprocity with their mother, Jutta. The later reciprocal talking of these pages is a form of exchange which emerges out of reciprocities already there.

Indeed, such was the richness of their earlier epoch, before the onslaught of language that our pleasure having our children to talk to us was tinged with sadness and nostalgia for the subtlety of their music and dance before they spoke. It's sometimes difficult to keep up with one's children: not to mourn, in gaining a girl, a boy, the loss of babyhood and infancy. And by the time this book is being read, the children depicted in its pages will already have grown out of their clothes several times.

Some of these conversations have struck some people as so incredible, that I've been asked if I made them up. No. I did not. I could not. However much I would like to lay claim to their invention I can vouch only for the fact that I have added nothing. I am responsible for deletions and, I suppose, inevitably, some inadvertent omissions. But I have made no additions, no embellishments. I have selected. There are intimacies within family life which I am old-fashioned enough to believe are unseemly to reveal publicly. Indeed I have hesitated for several years before coming to feel that it does not offend my sense of propriety in disclosing this much of a very private domain. This is done with the full accord of my wife – and the children.

Need I say also that the children have not spent their lives having conversations with me. Their relation to their mother, my wife, is only glimpsed in these pages, but that should be enough to reveal the supreme importance she has in this family's scheme of things.

Nevertheless, with those and other limitations, as far as I know, no similar anthology dialogues with children has been published.

R. D. Laing
June 1977

London	**March 1970**

Adam	have you a long pole?
Daddy	no sorry
Adam	or a ladder?
Daddy	what do you want it for?
Adam	I want to knock down the sun and break it in two and give mummy it to cook and we'll eat it
Daddy	but what will we do without the sun in the sky?
Adam	I don't like it
Daddy	what's wrong with it?
Adam	it's *boring*
Daddy	but the *sun*. I'm fond of the sun
Adam	I'll get another
Daddy	how?
Adam	I'll buy one
Daddy	where?
Adam	in Woolworths
Daddy	I'm glad I haven't got a ladder to reach the sun if that's what you would do with it
Adam	O *daddy*. (*pause*) haven't you got one I could stand on tiptoe on top of, and poke it out with a stick?

Ceylon	**April 1971**

Adam	(*on hearing of fighting, shooting and killing in Kandy, 14 miles away*) I want to go to Kandy and kill people and cut them up and eat them for breakfast with a big steel gun and a stiff trigger
Daddy	why?
Adam	because I want to shoot a lot of people and kill them so they'll be dead. Like I did last time
Daddy	how do you mean last time?
Adam	last time I was here
Daddy	here?
Adam	last time I was alive

1

Daddy	how do you know?
Adam	I remember. I was a soldier. I killed a lot of people
Daddy	really
Adam	did you kill a lot of people last time daddy?
Daddy	I don't think so
Adam	not recently?
Daddy	no
Adam	but did you kill a lot of people a long, long time ago?
Daddy	I may have but I can't remember
Adam	you can't remember! (*incredulously*)
Daddy	no
Adam	oh

India   December 1971

After a storm

| Adam | what's the decoration on the moon?
(*before I could answer*)
it's a man with a hammer. When it's a storm, that's when he's angry |

London   February 1973

I'm sitting in my armchair reading

Natasha walks in, stifling her sobs, clambers on my lap, positions herself upright, facing away, tilts her head fully back, and bursts into howls and howls and howls.

I make a move to cuddle her but she elbows my arms away, and when I tentatively touch the tips of her fingers by way of some gesture of consolation, she snatches them away, and her howls threaten to turn into shrieks, or even sckreechs. As her howls continue I have just time to check my impulses to ask her what's the matter, to hug her, stroke her, or offer words of comfort, before as she is lower-

2

ing her head and turning to look at me for the first time, her
last howl fades. In one smile she says hello, bye-bye, perhaps,
thanks daddy. With a sigh of completion, she gets down from
my lap, and without a word between us since she came in
and without looking back, she ambles out of the door, ready
for her next adventure.

February 1973

Before dinner

Natasha is holding her head and howling. Is it bleeding?
Does it need a stitch? No. Nothing serious.
Adam did it with his rifle, she says.

He denies it. Then says he didn't mean it. That means he did.
I take his rifle and guns away from him, and put them up on
the top of a high shelf next to the ceiling.

At dinner

He is going to pour a bucket of water over me when I am
asleep in bed.
He is going to phone the police because I have been nasty to
him and he knows their number.

He'll make a ladder and get his guns down.
And Natasha joins in, on *his* side.
She is going to cut my head off
and then cut my nose off
and

> 'I'll have a secret place
> and you won't be able to find me'

After dinner

Adam has found a way to get his rifle and guns down.
He comes into my room with his rifle

> 'I'm going to put it where I (*sic*)
> can't find it'

3

He puts it away
A little later he comes in with it again to show me

Adam	You might not believe me
Me	O I believe you. It's alright
Adam	No. You just might not believe me.
	I'll just show you

He goes off with the rifle again, to hide it once more where
he can't find it. In a few minutes he's back with the rifle,
showing me it, almost pedagogically, to make trebly sure I
believe it. He goes off. A little later he's back, dressed in a
green commando suit, with tin hat and rifle.

Adam	Order me about
Me	I'm trying to get some work done do you mind
Adam	aw come on order me about

I order him about
Attention. Quick March. Halt. Stand at ease. Shoulder arms.
Quick march . . .

It is hours later. Past their bedtime.
Adam and Natasha are drawing. Peace and Quiet
He has borrowed from me my tin of special pens, pencils, felt
tips and nibs

> Ah! Now he's just spilled the lot over the floor!
> Arrggh

February 1973

> The Grand Old Man bends a long way down,
> out of politeness (*so that his eyes are level with
> Natasha's*), and inquires, with kindly solemnity

	Do you like being you?
Natasha	yes I like being me. I'm a very nice girl, and a
	very intelligent girl, and everyone likes me.
	Even mummy likes me.

February 1973

Natasha	Daddy. Would you like Mummy to be your mummy?

March 1973

Adam	What are you reading?
Me	love poems
Adam	Haven't you any hate poems?
Me	I'm just trying to read these just now if you don't mind
Adam	(*with glee*) Why don't you write some *hate* poems?

22 April 1973

Jutta, Adam and Natasha are off to Stuttgart tomorrow to stay with Jutta's parents for a week.

Bedtime

Daddy	I'm sad you're going away Natasha
Natasha	I'm not sad today, I'll be sad tomorrow

Jutta and I haven't been getting on very well recently. Natasha has become interested in glue, and sellotape, in cutting things up and sticking them together.

Just now she is dashing from one wall of my room to the other, thudding against them

Ronnie	What are you doing?
Natasha	the heart
Ronnie	the heart?

Natasha	yes (*she continued thudding against the walls*)
Ronnie	and what does the heart do?
Natasha	the heart loves (*she stopped dashing and thudding*)
Ronnie	the heart loves?
Natasha	yes
Ronnie	who? what?
Natasha	the one heart loves many people
Ronnie	the one heart loves many?
Natasha	the one heart loves many many

July 1973

Adam	and how would you like it if – come on daddy, it's your turn
Daddy	if someone shoved spaghetti up your nose
Adam	and how would you like it if someone mixed up sand and water into some sort of cement and put it down your throat
Daddy	and how would you like it if someone put you in a large tub – as large as this room – of treacle
Adam	and how would you like it if I cut off your nose
Daddy	and how would you like it if I cut off your arms, and body, and legs, and head – where would you be then
Adam	there (*patting me there*) in my body and how would *you* like it if I cut your body into teeny weeny bits (*illustrating with right thumb and forefinger*) and cut these little bits into little bits
Daddy	(*split second's hesitation*)
Adam	(*before I can get my breath*) where would you be then?
Daddy	(*he's got me on the run*)
Adam	(*pressing home his advance*) you tell me
Daddy	I don't know

Adam	(*flash*)*
Daddy	I might be like space
Adam	(*flash*)
Daddy	or I might be finished
Adam	(*flash*)
Daddy	what do you think
Adam	(*flash*)
Daddy	do you remember?
Adam	(*flash*)
Daddy	do you know?
Adam	(*flash*)
Daddy	maybe finished
Adam	mmmm

October 1973

Natasha is bashing at a door with a shoe

Natasha	I want to kill a little thing, daddy
Daddy	Oh. That's not very nice How would you like it if someone wanted to kill you?
Natasha	I want to kill it I want to kill it I want to kill it and that will be the end of it

November 1973

Adam has been trying to wriggle out of
something

Jutta	you can't cheat me I'm smarter than you I can *see* and smell your farts!

*with both arms, and whole body – like a con-
ductor indicating a split second flash of silence

7

Evening

Jutta and I have had a quarrel, and she has gone to a party alone.

I am sitting, writing, in a bad mood.
Natasha comes into the room, and starts to fiddle with sellotape. She crumbles a length of it, and spirals it around.

Daddy	what are you doing?
Natasha	I want to make a sword
Daddy	(*testily*) You can't make a sword out of sellotape

I was annoyed she hadn't confirmed my theory that it was an umbilical cord. Still.

She takes two pieces of white paper, and folds each exactly alike

Natasha	this is mummy piece and this is daddy piece

She sellotapes them together and puts them on my desk

Natasha	This is for *both* of you
Daddy	thank you, Natasha

She takes four pieces of paper and the sellotape: goes away and comes back in a few minutes.

She has folded and sellotaped two sets of two pieces

Natasha	This one's for you (*giving it to me*), and this one's for mummy (*taking it with her to her room*)

Later the same evening

Adam, Natasha and I have been flying paper aeroplanes; now it's quiet. Adam is watching TV in the children's room

Natasha is sitting reflectively in my armchair I am sitting at my desk nearby

Natasha	Daddy?
Daddy	Yes Natasha
Natasha	maybe mummy'll be *serious* when she comes home
Daddy	how do you mean?
Natasha	maybe she'll be serious
Daddy	about what?
Natasha	maybe she'll *scream* (*pause*). At Adam.

November 1973

Natasha and I are throwing a paper aeroplane back and forward to each other.

When it goes straight to her, and she fails to catch it she cries
You missed me
and when it goes wide of me, and I fail to catch it she cries
You missed it

December 1973

Natasha wants sellotape for Xmas

December 1973

Adam is allowed, on his own, to play with a match box, to take matches out of the box and to strike matches.

Natasha is allowed, on her own, to play with a match box, to take matches out, but not to strike them.
Just now, she can, because I'm around.

Natasha   (*striking matches, blowing them out,
         and musing, disconsolately*)
         Striking is better than taking out

         Then, brightening up

         but I can *leave** more than Adam

December 1973

         I'm sitting writing
         Scraps have been occurring to me.

         I can't even see
         why a flea is so wee

Mummy   I can't even see
              let alone where I'll be
         when I die

         (*talking to myself*)
         Where shall I be when I die? (*pause*) I don't
         know
Natasha   (*rather primly, as though I should know better*)
         nor do I. Nor does anyone know that

December 1973

Jutta   The Emperor had the most beautiful palace in
         all the world so that all the people passing by
         would be sure to notice it
Natasha   I can't breathe

         *that is, on her plate

10

Jutta	I won't read anymore if you go on like that
Natasha	I'm holding my breath
Jutta	I'm finished. Put out the light
Natasha	I want it on
Jutta	put it out
Natasha	I want it on
Jutta	I'm not going to tell you a million times
Natasha	a million hurts me

1973

Natasha is holding onto one of my legs as I am standing lighting my pipe. I'm frightened some lighted ash or sparks will fall on her

Me	you shouldn't hold onto my leg when I'm lighting my pipe or you'll burn yourself
Natasha	you shouldn't hold onto someone's leg when you're lighting your pipe or you'll burn yourself

January 1974

Daddy	why did the peacock scream?
Adam	because he couldn't see himself
Natasha	because he wanted to hear himself

January 1974

Me	don't do that
Adam	I will if you won't let me

January 1974

Kira	Adam is following me
Me	why are you following her?
Adam	I follow her
	'cos she follows me

11

Natasha and Adam are very fond of smarties these days. They come to me for them. I gave them more than Jutta thinks is good for them.

Natasha   (*to Jutta*) I love daddy because he buys me smarties

Daddy   (*somewhat hurt*) is that why you love daddy?

Natasha   yes that's why I love you

a few days later

Natasha   have you any smarties?

Daddy   yes (*and gave her some*)

Natasha   and for Adam?

Daddy   I've got some for him too

She went away with them, and came back after she had eaten them.

Natasha   I love you daddy. I don't just love you because you bring me smarties. It's not just because you bring me smarties

January 1974

Afternoon

Natasha is hitting a wicket chair with a wooden hatchet made by Adam this afternoon

Daddy   Ok that's enough (*it goes on*) that's enough (*it goes on*) stop it (*she continues*) I'll take the hatchet away (*even harder bangs*) I'll take the hatchet away and put you out of the room

Natasha   I'll hit you in the eye first

Daddy   Ok

I wrest the hatchet out of her wrist and seize her wrist. I'm prepared to drag her out of the room. But she's already walking out herself and

just as I get to the door to slam it on her, she's
slammed it right on my face, flinging back at me
as she marches off

Now you've locked it For Ever and Ever

Evening

It's been somewhat hectic. A boxing match with
Adam. A tickling session with both of them. It's
quiet again, though I'm feeling a bit frayed, like
that wool lying around they've been using to
tie onto chair and table legs to stretch across the
floor in the hope of tripping people up. I gather
it up, slump on a chair, and, absently, wind it

Natasha	what do you think *you're* doing
Me	I'm winding up some wool
Natasha	you're winding up your*self*, *that's* what you're doing. You're winding up your*self* that's what *I* think you're doing

January 1974

Adam	what do shells do?
Daddy	they're like bombs. They explode and destroy. That's all.
Adam	but you can take the detonator out
Daddy	er, yes – you can. And if they can't explode anymore they can become an ornament. Like this.

This, is three shells (*a larger one, standing
upright, and two smaller ones*) arranged together as a crucifix with the figure of Christ
Crucified on the cross they form. I have it on
my mantelpiece

Daddy	You can do that with them
Adam	what's that?
Daddy	it's a man being crucified

13

Adam	what's 'crucified'?
Daddy	they used to make a large cross out of tree trunks, stick it in the ground and nail someone on it like that till they died
Adam	why did they do that to people?
Daddy	to punish people. They don't do that now
Adam	I know. They put them in gaol or treat them

Thursday   **23 January 1974**

Natasha	(*listening to the clavichord*) That's beautiful. That's very difficult, I can *easily* do very difficult things by practising

February 1974

Daddy	what was the first thing you saw when you came out of mummy's tummy?
Natasha	mummy's pussa, that's the first thing I saw when I came out of mummy's tummy
Daddy	and what was mummy's pussa like?
Natasha	mummy's pussa was like mummy's secret heart, that's what mummy's pussa was like
Daddy	and what was mummy's secret heart like?
Natasha	mummy's secret heart was like your two eyes, that's what mummy's secret heart was like
Daddy	and what are my two eyes like?
Natasha	your two eyes are like your nose, that's what your two eyes are like
Daddy	and what is my nose like?
Natasha	your nose's like your teeth, that's what your nose is like
Daddy	and what are my teeth like?
Natasha	your teeth are like your toes, that's what your teeth are like
Daddy	and what are my toes like?
Natasha	your toes are like your fingers,

14

	that's what your toes are like
Daddy	and what are my fingers like?
Natasha	your fingers are like your throat,
	that's what your fingers are like
Daddy	and what is my throat like?
Natasha	your throat is like between your knees,
	that's what your throat is like
Daddy	and what is between my knees like?
Natasha	between your knees is like between your eyes,
	that's what between your knees is like
Daddy	and what is between your eyes like?
Natasha	between your eyes is like your next head,
	that's what between your eyes is like
Daddy	and what is my next head like?
Natasha	don't be silly

22 March 1974

Old gentleman	what can Natasha do?
Natasha	I can blow up *most* balloons myself

Winter 1974

Daddy	Natasha. I have to go away for a little while
Natasha	can I come with you?
Daddy	no I have to go away by myself for a little while
Natasha	and you're coming back in a little while?
Daddy	yes
Natasha	alright daddy (*reflective silence*)
	but daddy?
Daddy	yes Natasha
Natasha	do you love me daddy?
Daddy	yes I do love you Natasha
Natasha	well if you love me you have to let
	me be near you
	you have to let me be near you if you
	love me

15

1 April 1974

Natasha	here is a present for you and Jutta
	it's for both of you
	it's a ball of wire
	I found the wire in the garden and I thought I
	would like to give you and Jutta a present so I
	made it into a ball
	it didn't take long
	you can play with it if you like
	you can throw it to each other if you like
	I don't mind if it falls,
	if it's an accident
	and I don't mind if it breaks,
	if it's an accident
	it's alright
	I'll fix it it won't take long
Me	thank you Natasha
	I'll put it here on my desk
Natasha	yes you must take care of it
	you can throw it to each other
	it's for *both* of you

27 April 1974

	two days ago
Adam	when do we go back to school
Jutta	the day after tomorrow
Adam	when is that?
Natasha	two sleeps

30 April 1974

Natasha is playing with Natasha

Natasha	(*to herself*) *fast*	
	(*pointing to her nose*)	this is my foot
	(*pointing to her eyes*)	this is my nose
	(*pointing to her foot*)	this is my eyes
	(*pointing to her mouth*)	this is my neck
	(*pointing to her bottom*)	this is my head
	(*pointing to her ankle*)	this is my wrist

pause
faster
my face is my tummy
my tummy's my eyes
my eyes are my tongue
my tongue is my ankles
my ankles are my hands
pause
cross your hands
cross your legs
cross your eyes
cross your nose
gurgles of amusement

11 June 1974

my study

Natasha (*with abrupt unsolicited finality*)
         there's no monster in *this* room
Daddy   Oh
Natasha No. I looked under the mat (*conclusively*)
Daddy   How could a monster be under the mat?

She looks at me as though I don't know *anything*

1 July 1974

Natasha   I don't need a night light anymore daddy
I'm not afraid of the dark anymore 'cos I don't
see pictures anymore

Daddy   a night light's still nice though
you don't have to be afraid to have one

Natasha   No. But I don't see pictures anymore

11 July 1974

Natasha   are you sad?

Jutta   yes

Natasha   are you sad about life?

Jutta   yes

Natasha   I still like you (*pause*)
shall I be your mummy?

Jutta   O Natasha

Natasha   I'll be your mummy and you can have
a rest for a little while, alright?

Jutta   alright

Natasha   alright

She gives Jutta a hug and a kiss and runs off.
She returns after a few minutes

I don't want to be your mummy anymore
Was that nice?

Jutta   yes. Thank you Natasha

Natasha   that's alright.
You a little less sad now?

Jutta   yes

15 July 1974

Jutta is crying and moaning in bed

Natasha	why are you crying mummy?
Jutta	I don't know
Natasha	are you crying about life?
Jutta	yes
	(*pause, sobs*)
Natasha	we're not going to die
Jutta	we'll all have to die sooner or later
Natasha	but we're not going to die *soon*
	we're not going to die till later.
	We'll die *later* (*comfortingly*)

31 July 1974

Dinner

I pour out meticulously, *exactly* the same amount of fruit juice for both

Natasha	I've got more than Adam

Jutta serves as far as humanly possible the same size of helping as Adam

Natasha	I've got more than Adam. Mine is more than Adam's
Adam	No it isn't
Natasha	yes it is (*tears*)

She ate hardly anything, and when Adam had immediately finished his plate, almost as fast as me, she announced, triumphantly

Natasha	I've *left* more than Adam

August 1974

Ever since Natasha has been putting her shoes on herself (for more than a year now), she has almost always put them on the 'wrong' feet.

It could not have been a random error.

A year ago, for two or three months, she *always* put them on the wrong feet, and refused to change them. This used to bother Jutta who would *insist* she change them before going out, and predicted dire consequences to her feet, and to her, if she didn't.

In the last few months, she has been coming into my room in the mornings and asking

'Is it right'

Occasionally it is, but usually it isn't

Last week is the first week ever, that they have been 'right' every time.

August 1974

	Bedtime. Tuck in. Say your Prayers
Adam	Ronnie?
Ronnie	yes
Adam	is it alright if I say
	'God bless God'
Ronnie	. . . er, yyyes, I suppose so
Adam	what does it mean?
Ronnie	I've no idea what it means
Adam	is it alright?
Ronnie	yes it's alright
Adam	goodnight Ronnie
Ronnie	goodnight Adam

1 September 1974

Adam	I'm frightened
Me	of what?
Adam	I said something, I don't know whether it's alright
Me	what did you say?
Adam	do you know the marriage ceremony?
Me	yes
Adam	I said a bit of it
Me	what bit?
Adam	I now pronounce you man and wife
Me	who did you say it to?
Adam	a doll
Me	what doll?
Adam	Natasha's little Japanese doll
Me	Natasha's little Japanese doll
Adam	will it be alright?
Me	yes it'll be alright

18 September 1974

Me	. . . and happy dreams, and don't forget your prayers
Natasha	and don't forget *your* prayers
Me	God bless
Natasha	(*interrupting*) God bless nothing. God bless nothing. God bless NOTHING
Adam	God bless God

20 October 1974

Natasha often asks me to do up her shoe or boot laces.
A few weeks ago I was doing them several times a day.
She specifies which foot first, what pattern, how firm, the type of knot, and the size of bow.
It all has to be precisely symmetrical.

Until the last two weeks it always had to be a double knot.
But now,

> you needn't do that now, daddy, it's alright, they don't make a sound anymore, you needn't do that, daddy, 'cos they don't make a sound anymore

27 October 1974

	Charlie is three
Natasha	Charlie hugs people because he doesn't like them. That's why he hugs them

9 November 1974

Natasha	you can't tie your two shoe laces at once because you can't do two times at once

1974

Natasha	how long does forty minutes take?

Adam	there's going to be three of us
Daddy	yes
Adam	mummy's going to have a baby
	(*pause*)
	aren't you proud of her?
Daddy	yes
Adam	yes

Monday   **25 November 1974**

Evening

Natasha	why are you looking down?
Ronnie	I'm feeling sad
Natasha	why are you feeling sad?
Ronnie	I don't know
Natasha	you don't know
Ronnie	I want to write things, but I don't seem able to
Natasha	why are you not able to?
Ronnie	I don't know
Natasha	what do you want to write?
Ronnie	I want to tell people what people tell me
Natasha	maybe you can't remember what people tell you. Maybe you've forgotten what people tell you
Ronnie	well. You hear a *lot* of what people tell me. Can *you* remember what people tell me?*
Natasha	yes. I can remember
Ronnie	people say so many things
Natasha	yes I know
Ronnie	and what do they say?
Natasha	they want to go home

*Natasha is only allowed into my room when I'm seeing people if I don't know she's there. She has a pair of Tibetan house-shoes she calls 'sneakers', which make no sound and usually make her invisible. She puts them on to sneak into my room and curl up under my desk

Ronnie	Oh. Really
Natasha	yes. They want to go home
Ronnie	but they don't know how to go home
Natasha	I know
Ronnie	how can they go home, if they don't know the way home?
Natasha	I don't know
Ronnie	how can I tell them?
Natasha	I don't know
Ronnie	that's why I'm so sad
Natasha	Daddy?
Ronnie	Natasha?
Natasha	are you going to write that down?
Ronnie	yes
Natasha	I knew you would
Ronnie	it's difficult isn't it?
Natasha	if they spent the night here, they would find their house
Ronnie	(*silence*)
Natasha	you're not going to write that down are you?
Ronnie	probably not
Natasha	I thought you wouldn't (*disapprovingly*)

Sunday   1 December 1974

Sitting on my lap

Natasha	you can't remember one thing
Ronnie	Oh. What?
Natasha	there's lots of things you can remember but there's one thing you can't remember
Ronnie	Oh. There's lots and lots of things I can't remember
Natasha	I know. But there's one thing you can't remember
Ronnie	what is the one thing I can't remember?
Natasha	you were in here talking to one of the people who come to see you

24

Ronnie	what was it?
Natasha	(*laughing*) I don't know
Ronnie	if you don't know what is the one thing I can't remember how do you know I can't remember it?
Natasha	what did you say?
Ronnie	if you don't know what is the one thing I can't remember how do you know I can't remember it?
Natasha	I don't know
Ronnie	you don't know how you know there's one thing I can't remember?
Natasha	no
Ronnie	then how can you say that then?
Natasha	there's one thing I do know
Ronnie	Oh. what's that?
Natasha	first lady forward, second lady back first lady's finger up the second lady's crack
Ronnie	Oh really? and is there nothing else you know?
Natasha	(*slowly*) Septimus Branigan he was there He put up a magnificent show He shoved his tagger up his arse And tied it in a bow
Ronnie	Oh is there nothing else you know than that?
Natasha	I'm going to tell Adam something I'll be back (*she runs off and comes back shortly*) I forgot one
Ronnie	don't tell me
Natasha	landing on her tits
Ronnie	I don't want to talk about it
Natasha	do you remember it?
Ronnie	yes
Natasha	do you still remember it?
Ronnie	yes
Natasha	say it then
Ronnie	I really don't want to. I'm sorry I told you these ones
Natasha	come on Daddy

Ronnie	the minister's wife she was there
	she had us all in fits
	jumping off the mantelpiece
Natasha	and landing on her tits
	and landing on her tits
	and landing on her tits
	(*peals of laughter*)

She runs off and comes back in a few seconds

	I've made up a few
Ronnie	Oh really? what?
Natasha	two tomatoes crossing the road
Ronnie	you never made that up you heard it from someone
Natasha	no I didn't. I made that one up
Ronnie	I'd heard it before
Natasha	No you haven't
	I made that one up myself

And off she runs again

December 1974

After midnight

Natasha comes into my room trailing her quilt. It's dark apart from a desk lamp. She stands silently for a while.

Natasha	When are you going to bed daddy?
Daddy	(*testily*) I don't know. Why?
Natasha	I'm not going to bed till you go to bed
Daddy	(*gruffly*) you can go to bed whenever you like as long as I don't know you're up. I just want to work I don't want to hear you or see you anymore tonight, alright?
Natasha	alright you'll have to carry me out
Daddy	I'm sorry Natasha. I don't feel like it
Natasha	that's the only way you'll get me out of the room

Daddy	No
Natasha	and you'll have to carry me all the way to my bed and snuggle me in
Daddy	(*softening*) alright as long as this is the last time. This is definitely the last time tonight
Daddy	(*picking her up*) promise
Natasha	(*being carried*) promise
Daddy	(*tuggling her in*) you promised before
Natasha	I know. The last time was the very very last time
Daddy	and this is the very very very last time
Natasha	(*snuggling in*) say your prayers
Daddy	(*kissing her*) I mean it this time. Goodnight Natasha
Natasha	(*as Daddy is walking away – calling out*) say your prayers
Daddy	(*at the door – in a loud whisper*) yes I will. And you say your prayers
Natasha	goodnight Daddy
Daddy	goodnight Natasha

11 December 1974

Natasha opens the door of my room and ushers in Charlie. He slumps against the wall whimpering

Me	what's the matter Charlie?
Charlie	(*eventually*) I'm afraid of the Chinese puzzle
Me	Why?
Charlie	(*eventually*) there are baddies in it
Me	how do you mean?
Charlie	there are baddies in it
Natasha	I gave it to the cat
Me	What! The Chinese puzzle!
Natasha	Yes. I gave it to the cat. It's alright Charlie

Charlie ran off, looking more scared than ever

Me	what did he mean?

Natasha	how?
Me	when he said there were baddies in it
Natasha	it's a *Chinese* puzzle
Me	well?
Natasha	the Chinese are baddies
Me	he thought there were actual baddies actually inside the Chinese puzzle
Me	you told him
Natasha	no I didn't
Me	and now he'll think there are actual Chinese baddies inside the cat!
Natasha	no he will not
Me	anyhow why do you say the Chinese are baddies?
Natasha	I heard it on television
Me	really
Natasha	they are baddies because they kill people
Me	there are some baddies everywhere
Natasha	the Chinese are some baddies
Me	there are some baddies everywhere
Natasha	no there're not

17 December 1974

Dinner

A lady is yattering on and on

Natasha	do you hear what you're saying
Lady	No (*startled*) Thank God! (*giggle*)
Natasha	(*severely*) if you wiggle your ear with every mind in you your chair might go up

December 1974

Car drive from London to Devon

Adam and Natasha will not stop squabbling, squawking, squawling in the back seat

Jutta	if you don't shut up, I'm going to leave the pair of you
Natasha	well go ahead then
Jutta	just don't be so cheeky
Natasha	I'm going to run away
Jutta	well run away then
Natasha	how can I run away when I don't know where I am?

5 January 1975

Natasha	I hope I'm dead when I die

Monday **16 February 1975**

Natasha	what am I?
Daddy	you're half German
Mummy	and half Scottish
Natasha	half German?
Mummy	and the other half of you is Scottish
Natasha	what is the whole of me?
Mummy	you're a funny mixture (*laughing*)
Natasha	(*hitting Jutta with a piece of paper*)
	I'm not friends with you
Jutta	Oh Natasha
Natasha	it's not funny at all
Jutta	I'm not laughing *at* you
Natasha	yes you were
Jutta	not in *that* way
Natasha	I'm not friends with you
Jutta	I'm not laughing *at* you

Natasha	yes you were I don't like you any more
Ronnie	there's one from mummy
	and one from daddy
	and the two of them become one
	and the whole of that one is you
Jutta	it's absolutely terrifying
Ronnie	what is?
Jutta	crushing all that into one

Natasha left the room and came back in a little
while with two pieces of paper, out of the
middle of each of which she had cut two circles

Natasha	here is one hole for you (*giving one piece to Jutta*) and here's one hole for you (*giving one piece to me*)
Jutta } Ronnie }	Oh thank you Natasha
Natasha	(*to Jutta*) I give up the fight
	and they are friends again

3 April 1975

Adam is standing looking seriously puzzled

Daddy	what is it?
Adam	this stairway wasn't even *here*,
	until they put it here

22 May 1975

Natasha	God bless mummy and daddy and
	Adam and Natasha and
	God bless everything. Good-bye

Evening

Natasha	what's that book
Ronnie	that's the Bible
Natasha	what's the Bible?
Ronnie	it's a book of stories about God and us
Natasha	does it tell stories about God?
Ronnie	yes
Natasha	are these stories about God?
Ronnie	they are stories that some people say are about God
Natasha	are they *really* about God?
Ronnie	I don't know
Natasha	will you read me one?

I read her the first twenty-two verses of Genesis

Natasha	is it all about God?
Ronnie	yes
Natasha	has this page got God in it? (*leafing through the pages and picking out pages at random*)
Ronnie	yes
Natasha	and this page?
Ronnie	yes
Natasha	and this page?
Ronnie	yes
Natasha	and this page?
Ronnie	yes
Natasha	I think God is on every page
Ronnie	He's given different names but He can't really have a name we cannot really name Him
Natasha	I know, he's not a girlie (*pause*) nor a boy (*pause*) you don't know whether He's a boy or a girl do you?
Ronnie	no

Natasha	no one knows God but He knows us,
	and He knows Himself
Ronnie	how do you know that?
Natasha	I don't know how I know it
Ronnie	but you know it
Natasha	Yes. And no one can see God
	but He can see us and
	He can see Himself
	He could be in this house
	He could be outside the door
	He could knock on the door
	but He would have to knock very hard
	for us to hear Him, wouldn't he?
Ronnie	yes
Natasha	No we don't hear the God-knocks (*with a sad chuckle*)
	He would have to knock on the *God*-door!
Ronnie	and where shall we say the God-door is?
Natasha	how would someone like me know where the God-door is?
Ronnie	do you think God minds us talking about Him like this?
Natasha	No. He doesn't mind
	(*pause*)
	maybe we can see *through* Him,
	like your glasses (*laughing, seriously, quizzically*)
	(*pause*)
	do you think so?
Ronnie	I don't know (*pause*)
	see *through* Him but not see Him (*musing*)
Natasha	He can see Himself. We can't see Him.
	Some *gods* can see Him. He can see us.
	(*she is leafing through the Bible as she is saying this*)
	I can't look at every page tonight otherwise I'll get to stay up late and be tired so I'll go now daddy
Ronnie	alright Natasha

We are in a large delightful bedroom. Natasha
had earlier brought up a spray of flowers
'These are for you and Jutta.' Now, after the
foregoing conversation, she sits on the bed, in
silence, contemplating me on the floor, surrounded with sheaves of paper, reading what I
have been writing, scoring out, tearing up,
cutting and piecing together, arranging and re-
arranging.

Natasha	you've done an awful lot of writing
Ronnie	I know
Natasha	I think you've almost finished your book*
Ronnie	I'm very glad to hear it. I sure hope so
	Are you sure?
Natasha	yes. you've almost finished it
	(*kisses*)
	I'm going downstairs now
Ronnie	alright. thanks for the flowers
	goodnight
Natasha	I'm not going to bed, but you can say good-
	night if you want to
Ronnie	goodnight Natasha
Natasha	goodnight Ronnie

Sunday   **25 May 1975**

Natasha	can I jump on you?
David	yes
Natasha	are you sure?
David	yes
Natasha	I'm five now you know not four and three
	quarters

*She was right. I was almost at the end of what
turned out to be *The Facts of Life*.

33

Natasha	Tony says his father is a giant.
	he is bigger than Joan (*her teacher*)
Me	is he bigger than me?
Natasha	I don't know

She has been measuring people's heights by a length of string and a tape rule. She wants me to tell her how many of my hands' length she is. She is seven of my hands long.

July 1975

Natasha explains to Adam

Harry can't marry his mummy and
Lucy can't marry her daddy and
you can't marry me

Sunday   27 July 1975

Natasha persuaded Jutta recently to buy her a small screwdriver. It is nicely proportioned with a blue handle

Natasha	do you like my screwdriver?
Ronnie	yes I do. It's very sweet
Natasha	do you think it's *very* sweet?
Ronnie	yes. It's very pretty
Natasha	it's the *smallest* screwdriver in the house. Isn't it? Is it the smallest screwdriver in the house?
Ronnie	it might well be. I'm not absolutely sure
Natasha	if you need to screw anything, you can use it. I'll let you use it whenever you want to
Ronnie	thank you very much

Natasha	will you keep it for me?
Ronnie	alright. we can put it on my desk, and you can take it whenever you like
Natasha	alright

She left it on my desk for a few days, sometimes taking it away, and putting it back. Then she has kept it herself. Last night she went to bed with it.

| Natasha | (*as Jutta is tuggling in*)
I'm going to sleep with my little screwdriver. Thank you for giving my little screwdriver. I like it. It's the smallest one in the whole house |

Tuesday   29 July 1975

Early evening

Jutta and I are sitting around talking with friends Natasha comes in the room with boxing gloves on, and a pair for me.

Natasha	will you have a boxing match?
Ronnie	no not just now. I'm talking just now. I don't feel like it just now
Natasha	will you have a boxing match later?
Ronnie	well, maybe
Natasha	you have a boxing match with me later, when you don't need to talk, alright Daddy? You have a boxing match with me when you don't *need* to talk anymore. Alright Daddy?
Ronnie	alright Natasha
Natasha	I might marry Matthew (*reflective pause*) And if he won't marry me, I might marry Anthony (*another reflective pause*) And if he won't marry me, I might marry Andrew (*long pause*)

35

Ronnie	and if he wouldn't marry you, whom would you marry?
Natasha	if he wouldn't marry me, I might marry – Michael
Ronnie	and if he wouldn't marry you?
Jutta	you haven't mentioned Charlie
Natasha	Mmmmmmm. I'll marry who I like

4 August 1975

Natasha wants me to make her a bow with a stick of wood and a length of string.
While I'm fixing it

Natasha	am I allowed a piece of wood that's longer than my arm?
Ronnie	why not? this is about the length of your arm, isn't it?
Natasha	but am I?
Ronnie	what?
Natasha	*allowed* it if it's *longer* than my arm?
Ronnie	I suppose so. There's no rule against it, as far as I know. So yes. You're allowed it

She still looks unconvinced

August 1975

Jutta is cradling Max

Natasha	(*softly and sweetly to herself, but loud enough for Jutta to hear her*)
	I have a lovely mummy I have a kind mummy
	I have a beautiful mummy called Jutta
	(and then with no pause, suddenly, in a sharp peremptory tone)
	Have you put new sheets in my bed?
Jutta	not yet. I will. Later.

Natasha	are you putting Max in *my* bed?
Jutta	yes
Natasha	(*reproachfully*) you usuallly put him in *Adam's* bed
Jutta	(*on the defensive*) not always
Natasha	and you said I could hold him as well as Adam and you let Adam hold him and not me and it's not fair

Jutta without a word handed Max to Natasha

Natasha	(*rocking Max*) you're beautiful
	I think you're a queen
	everyone wouldn't
	I think you're beautiful
	I think you're a queen
	everyone wouldn't
Ronnie	you think he's a what?
Natasha	I don't want to tell you
Ronnie	a queen?
Natasha	yes

I shouldn't have said anything. She started to sing him 'My Grandfather's Clock'.

9 August 1975

| Jutta | (*To Adam and Natasha in a quiet commanding voice which brooked no nonsense*) |
| | Tidy your beds, straighten your pillows, fold your sheets |

They set about it.

Adam	you're just doing this because you have to
Natasha	No. I'm doing it because I want to
Adam	you're doing it because you have to
Natasha	No. I'm doing it because I want to
Adam	mummy told us to so we have to
Natasha	I still don't have to if I don't want to

Adam	Oh yes you do
Natasha	no I don't
Adam	you have to
Natasha	I don't have to I want to

Thursday 14 August 1975

Adam has just come into the room with two model aircraft he has made. After Jutta and I had admired them

Adam	I like this one better
Ronnie	why?
Adam	because *this* one (*the other one*) is only a civilian plane
Ronnie	what's wrong with that?
Adam	it doesn't carry any rockets
Ronnie	it's a very nice design
Adam	Oh I like the design of it. But it's only got these bombs (*pointing to two under each wing*) and they are only to be used if *absolutely* necessary
Jutta	rockets and bombs aren't particularly beautiful
Adam	well I like this one better because it's a *war* plane

Saturday 16 August 1975

Jutta gave Natasha a present of a large (neither inflatable nor deflatable), many-coloured ball a few days ago

For the last three days, first thing on waking she has come into our (*Jutta's, my and Max's*) bedroom, with the ball, complaining that it is getting smaller.

Natasha	the ball is smaller
Jutta	no it's not Natasha. It's exactly the same size

Natasha	no. The ball is getting smaller
Ronnie	you're getting bigger every day,
	so the ball may seem to you to be
	getting smaller
Jutta	she is growing at such a rate
	these days
Natasha	the ball is getting smaller

August 1975

Natasha	why did the boy throw the clock out
	the window?
Adam	because he wanted to see time fly*

Devon   **August 1975**

It's a sultry summer's day by a waterfall.
Natasha is sitting naked on a rock, singing to herself

> I'm going away
> I'm sad to say
> for many a day
> (*pause*)
>
> I'm going away
> for many a day
> unless you call
> (*longer pause, but not very long*)
>
> Please don't call
> for I want to stay
>   away
> for many a day

*A patient of mine once ate her favourite record
I asked Jutta
Why did that girl eat the record?
| Jutta | because she wanted the music inside her |

39

Devon   **August 1975**

Hot Summer's morning

I am absorbed in reading and brooding over *The Agamemnon* of Aeschylus, deep in the labyrinth of that dark legend.

Someone is tugging my beard.

>   Daddy?

Natasha must have been standing there for some time

>   Daddy? (*twirling my beard*) Have you forgotten
>   how to smile daddy?
>   Ah! That's a smile. Cheerio daddy

Tuesday   **26 August 1975**

Natasha	can you pick up David?
Ronnie	yes
Natasha	and can David pick up you?
Ronnie	yes
Natasha	you can pick up David and David can pick up you?
Ronnie	yes
Natasha	and what about Arthur?
Ronnie	David can pick up Arthur and Arthur can pick up David
Natasha	and what about you?
Ronnie	Arthur can pick up me and I can pick up Arthur
Natasha	Oh

Wednesday **27 August 1975**

Natasha	(*contemplating Max*) now I'm not the littlest one anymore

40

August 1975

Natasha has become intrigued by a cubical box.
She has been turning it around looking at it curiously, from all angles.

Now she has cut out two of its sides, and has been showing it to everyone around. She is fairly jumping with excitement.

> Look daddy. If you look *through* it,
> you can't see the bottom of it

Devon	**August 1975**
Natasha	I've found a wiggly tooth
Daddy	let me feel it. O yes
Natasha	yes that's the naughty tooth. I'm not going to tell anyone about it
Daddy	why not?
Natasha	I've told everyone here about it. But I'm not going to tell anyone in London about it
Daddy	No?
Natasha	No. Because it's a secret and if I told everyone about it, it wouldn't be a secret anymore, would it?
Daddy	no I suppose it wouldn't

Monday	**1 September 1975**
	At breakfast
Adam	when I'm ten you'll be eight and when I'm thirteen you'll be eleven because I'm two years older than you
Natasha	I can't get older than you but I can get bigger than you
Adam	you can get bigger than me but I doubt it
Natasha	you doubt it
Adam	Yes. I doubt it

41

Morning

Jutta	would you go over to the house and bring back a bottle of milk and some butter please Adam

Adam continues doing what he is doing

Jutta	Adam! how many times do I have to ask you to do something
Adam	what?
Jutta	would you go over to the house and bring a bottle of milk and some butter please
Adam	No
Jutta	Ronnie!
Ronnie	what?
Jutta	I've asked Adam twice to do something and he just won't do it
Ronnie	to do what?
Jutta	to go and get milk and butter from the house
Ronnie	didn't you hear mummy ask you?
Adam	yes but I don't have to
Ronnie	she was *asking* you nicely, I'm *telling* you
Adam	you mean I can't refuse
Daddy	you can refuse, but if you do I'll be very unpleasant to you
Adam	in what way?
Daddy	in *some* way
Adam	in *what* way?
Daddy	just do it
Adam	but in *what* way?
Daddy	you won't get any biscuits today

He started calculating. My eyes narrowed. My tone changed

just get moving or you're in big trouble with me right now

Adam	you mean I've got to
Daddy	yes

He went

In a compartment on the train

Natasha	I've cleaned my hands, can I touch Max?
Ronnie	no
Natasha	ho ho ho. Yes
Ronnie	no
Natasha	Ronnie said no is yes
	yes is no
	ho ho ho
	no means yes
	and yes means no
	Ronnie said yes
Ronnie	*No* Natasha
Natasha	alright daddy

September 1975

Playing ball with Natasha

Daddy	three more throws
Natasha	six more

after three more

Natasha	three more
Daddy	well alright

after these three more

Natasha	one more
Daddy	well this is the last one

after the last one

Natasha	one more
Daddy	well this is the very last one

after the very last one

Natasha	one more
Daddy	well this is the very very last one

43

after the very very last one

Natasha   I'm running off now

And away she ran with never a glance behind
her
No very very very last time

London   **September 1975**

Evening

Suddenly I was tired. I had to stretch out. Just
as I lay down

Natasha   will you untie my balloon?
Daddy   sorry Natasha I'm tired
Natasha   but I want you to untie my balloon
Daddy   later, in about ten minutes maybe but not now
Natasha   Ooh daddy but I want you to do it now
Daddy   sorry not now not now. I've got to shut my eyes
and not move *anything* for a few minutes
(*silence*)
Natasha   do you think one balloon is enough?
Daddy   it depends what for
Natasha   when it's my birthday would you buy me one
balloon?

Adam's birthday was yesterday. There had been
dozens of balloons at his birthday party

Daddy   Oh I would get you a *packet* of balloons
As many as Adam. More if you want
Natasha   and how many would you get me if it
wasn't my birthday?
Daddy   I would get you a packet of balloons
if you really wanted anytime
Natasha   but do you think one's enough?

I was puzzled. I said nothing

Natasha   I think one's enough

Then she burst the one she was holding.
Accidently. I startled.

Oh sorry daddy
Oh I popped my balloon! sorry
daddy (*and she ran off to mummy*)
mummy I popped my balloon, mummy I
popped my balloon

Saturday   13 September 1975

Natasha   can everyone in the whole world
               smile?

Thursday   18 September 1975

Adam   I might just make one of my inventions
Ronnie   what inventions?
Adam   I have made many inventions
Ronnie   how many?
Adam   many
Natasha   four
Ronnie   and what are they?
Adam   my first invention was a space capsule
           with many capabilities
Ronnie   oh yes
Adam   and my second invention was a darikrex
Ronnie   a what?
Adam   a da – ikrex*
Ronnie   I have never heard of a darikrex
Adam   I invented the name
Ronnie   and what is it
Adam   it's a machine that shoots out of three tubes
Ronnie   shoots what out?

*the following day (19 September) there was a
report in the I.T.H. on work by Drs Herbert and Irving Dardik
on umbilical cord transplant surgery

45

Adam	bananas, peas and tomatoes
Ronnie	really!?
Adam	and my third invention was a carriage for crushing snow. It will have a specially designed cabin
Jutta	will it be cold?
Adam	it will be centrally heated, to avoid having to use electricity.

Tuesday 7 October 1975

Morning

Natasha	daddy
Daddy	yes Natasha
Natasha	I still don't know how to do knots in shoes
Daddy	you soon will
Natasha	I know. But Daddy. I put my shoe on *before* Adam

Evening

Natasha	(*swishing her arm*) does a car go faster than that
Daddy	yes. I think so. I'm not sure, actually
Natasha	how fast does my arm go?
Daddy	I'm not sure

Wednesday 4 November 1975

As we were sitting around the table with friends after dinner Natasha came in with a bottle

Natasha	look
Ronnie	Oh
Natasha	do you like my bottle
Ronnie	it's alright

46

Natasha	I'm collecting bottles
Ronnie	oh why?
Natasha	so I'll have *more* than Adam
Ronnie	how interesting. And what else is 'More than Adam?'
Natasha	after I've had a bath. I pour *more* water over my hair
Ronnie	really I didn't know that
Natasha	and I'm going to fill all my bottles up with water
Ronnie	then you'll *have more* water than Adam
Natasha	yes (*clinching it*)

Wednesday 12 November 1975

Late afternoon

As I was walking home I met Natasha and Matthew. Natasha said 'Hello Daddy'. We kissed. I walked on hearing her say to Matthew 'That's my daddy.'

About thirty minutes later, Natasha came in the bathroom while I was having a bath. She stood looking at me. And continued to stand looking.

Daddy	Well?
Natasha	are you the same daddy I kissed in the street?
Ronnie	(*irritably*) yes (*pause*) YES! Why?
Natasha	are you the same daddy?
Ronnie	YES! why? Do you think I may not be?
Natasha	your hair is shorter
Ronnie	yes it's shorter
Natasha	it's *grown* shorter (*doubtfully*)
Ronnie	no it hasn't grown shorter (*pause*) I had it *cut* shorter (*she doesn't believe me. I feel a pang of panic*) yes! It's true. There was a

man in here (*the first time this has ever hap-*
pened) who cuts hair.
He just cut my hair before you came home

Natasha   No *I* see. It *looks* shorter because you have
shampoo on.
(*That's a relief. At least she's discarded the
theory that I'm a different daddy*)

Ronnie   yes. But it is *actually* shorter
because it was *cut* shorter

Natasha   No. I see. It *looks* shorter and
you *look* different

And she went out the bathroom

Wednesday 12 November 1975

Adam   what did one candle say to the other
candle?
Daddy   I don't know
Adam   I'm going out tonight

Tuesday 18 November 1975

Evening

Jutta   (*teasing*) I'm going away
Adam   (*laughing*) you can't do that because I love you
and if you go away I'll kill you

November 1975

Same evening. Later

Natasha   I wish I could marry you daddy
Daddy   Oh Natasha. We can't
Natasha   I know because you're married to mummy
Daddy   even if I weren't, we couldn't

48

	because you're my daughter and I'm your daddy and daughters and daddys aren't allowed to get married
Natasha	we're in the same family
Daddy	yes
Natasha	but mummy's in the same family, so how can you be married to her?
Daddy	when mummy and I met she wasn't your mummy and we were not members of the same family and she isn't my daughter so it was alright to get married and have children
Adam	by putting your penis into mummy's vagina
Daddy	and become a family and get married
Jutta	it's bedtime now
Daddy	yes it's past your bedtime
Natasha	but I'm not sleepy
Daddy	I never said you were. Anyway. Kisses. (*kisses*) and you're to go through to your room and be quiet
Adam	(*kissing Jutta*) Natasha would like to marry daddy, and I would like to marry you.

20 November 1975

I am sitting reading Lovejoy's *The Great Chain of Being*.
Natasha is holding Max, whirling around.
Jutta announces 'Dinner!'

Natasha yells 'Charge!' and sets off at a gallop, but stops
after three or four steps

> Sorry Max. I didn't know I had you in my arms.
> Charge!

And resumes her gallop, this time holding Max, as she says
these days 'knowingly' or 'rememberingly'.

At dinner

Natasha	(*to Jutta and me*) were you two born together?
Ronnie	did we come out of the same mummy at the same time?
Natasha	yes
Ronnie	no we were born at different times, different places, and came out of two different mummies who are your two grannies

TV war film

Adam	change it
Jutta	keep it on I want to see it
Adam	you killer-lover!

Monday   **1 December 1975**

Adam	what is black and white and red all over
Natasha	I don't know
Adam	a newspaper
Natasha	it's not red all over
Adam	of course it's read all over

But Natasha didn't 'get it', quite.

2 December 1975

Adam	let's do a hand stand
Natasha	Oh yes that's what I was thinking of twenty-five years ago

8 December 1975

Natasha	are you older than Margaret
Jutta	yes Margaret is two weeks younger than me I think
Natasha	how old are you?
Jutta	I'm thirty-six
Natasha	are you older than Adam?
Jutta	of course I am, Natasha
Natasha	I'm not the youngest in this house now. Even if Max gets older he'll never get older than me. I'll always be older than him won't I mummy?
Jutta	yes Natasha
Natasha	is daddy older than Arthur?
Jutta	yes Natasha

December 1975

Xmas

Adam	(*exulting after two glasses of wine*) Come to Heaven!
Natasha	don't be silly, Heaven is dead!

January 1976

I'm in the bath. Natasha is standing beside it

Natasha	(*pointing to my right knee*) what's that?
Ronnie	that's a birthmark
Natasha	what's it for?
Ronnie	it's just there. My dad had one on *his* right knee
Natasha	what did you want it for?
Ronnie	I didn't want it. I just got it

She says nothing. She is not persuaded

you've got brown eyes. You've just got them

51

Natasha	but I *wanted* brown eyes
Ronnie	and that's why you got them?
Natasha	yes
Ronnie	Oh

I pondered over this information for a little
Well, is there anything about you you didn't want?

Natasha	no
Ronnie	you wanted to be a girlie and not a boyie?
Natasha	(*indignantly*) yes
Ronnie	nothing at *all* you didn't want?

Natasha's eyes roll right up so I see only their whites, as she scans all the possibilities. After a long pause

Natasha	I didn't want to be itchy

February 1976

As I'm setting off for a Chinese restaurant to bring a meal back for the family

Natasha	will you give me a carry on your shoulders?
Ronnie	Oh yes. But it's a cold winter's night outside
Natasha	I know. Will there be ghosts?
Ronnie	there may be
Natasha	there may be ghosts out there?
Ronnie	have you ever met a ghost?
Natasha	no
Ronnie	how do you know?
Natasha	I know
Ronnie	but if you've never met a ghost, how do you know what a ghost is like?
Natasha	I know
Ronnie	what's a ghost like?
Natasha	it's white, and it scares people. The white comes up from under it
Ronnie	Oh

Natasha	if it comes down *to* its feet it's not a ghost
Ronnie	how do you know that?
Natasha	I've seen it on television
Ronnie	Oh come on! most of what's on the television is just what people make up – it's not necessarily *true*
Natasha	Oh but I know that if it has white over it down to its ankles it isn't a real ghost
Ronnie	that's correct. You don't know how you know that, or do you?
Natasha	no I don't
Ronnie	but you know it?
Natasha	yes
Ronnie	you know quite a lot of things I don't know
Natasha	I know
Ronnie	and there's quite a lot you know and don't know that you know it
Natasha	I know
Ronnie	I don't think I know more than you know

Later, coming out of the restaurant

Natasha	the sky is red
Ronnie	I wish there weren't these streetlights then we could really see the sky
Natasha	I wish the sky was down here
Ronnie	and then? then we could fly on it
Natasha	I would lie on it

Saturday	**14 February 1976**

Natasha and Adam have been quarrelling

Natasha	I wish he were dead
Jutta	Oh Natasha
Natasha	I wish his seed had been crushed and he never had been
Jutta	but Natasha! Adam's your brother and you would miss him
Natasha	I *want* to miss him

Sunday	**14 March 1976**

This morning Natasha was angry at Jutta and me because we shouted at her for shouting

Natasha	(*to Jutta*) why do you have to lie like that?
Jutta	I don't lie
Natasha	you tell a lie every day
Jutta	no I don't
Natasha	you tell millions of lies
Ronnie	what lies?
Natasha	I'm not telling you anything

I had promised Adam and Natasha I would give them some sweets if.

Natasha	daddy when are we going to get some sweets?
Daddy	when mummy comes back
Natasha	is she bringing them back?
Daddy	no. When mummy comes back I'll give you and Adam some money to go out and get some sweets
Natasha	you cheat!
Daddy	why?
Natasha	you said you would *give* us the sweets

Daddy	ok when mummy comes back I'll go out and get some sweets, and bring them back and give them to you and Adam – is that all right?
Natasha	yes
Daddy	if you take care of Max till mummy comes back ok?
Natasha	yes

We each kept our side of the bargain

Tuesday   **April 1976**

Last night

Natasha	are you staying upstairs?
Daddy	no I think I'll go downstairs in about two minutes
Natasha	I thought you were going to say that
Daddy	you could stay up here
Natasha	no I'll stay with you. Where you go I'll go if you go downstairs I'll go downstairs if you go upstairs I'll go upstairs
Daddy	you could stay upstairs when I go downstairs
Natasha	then I'll get a creepy feeling
Daddy	what sort of creepy feeling?
Natasha	a creepy feeling like there was a ghost upstairs
Daddy	what sort of a ghost?
Natasha	a *real* ghost

Devon   **9 April 1976**

Evening

Natasha	when are we going home?
Daddy	the day after tomorrow
Natasha	when is that?
Daddy	it's tonight and
Natasha	two sleeps

Daddy	it's tonight and one sleep
Natasha	it's two sleeps in all
Daddy	you sleep tonight that's one sleep
	and then it's tomorrow. At the end
	of tomorrow you have another sleep
	and when you wake up from *that* sleep
	it's the day *after* tomorrow and that's
	the day we go home
Natasha	I have a sleep tonight for tomorrow
	and another sleep for the day we go home.
	That's two sleeps
Daddy	right
	do you know what's the name of tomorrow?
Natasha	no
Daddy	do you want me to tell you?
Natasha	yes
Daddy	the name of tomorrow is Saturday
Natasha	Oh Saturday
Daddy	Yes. And do you know the name of the
	day after tomorrow?
Natasha	No. What is it?
Daddy	Sunday
Natasha	Sunday

April 1976

Natasha	why did the ink run?
Daddy	I don't know
Natasha	because it was a repelling pencil
Daddy	a what?
Natasha	a *repelling* pencil
Daddy	I've never heard of a *repelling* pencil
Natasha	I know you haven't
	Later
Natasha	have you written that one down?
Daddy	no
Natasha	are you going to?

Daddy	well I'm not quite sure about it
Natasha	it was a repelling pencil
Daddy	but it doesn't sound quite the same as the others
Adam	like what's the quickest way to double your money?
Daddy	fold it
Adam	why do birds fly south?
Natasha	because it's too far to walk
Adam	what is a sleeping bull?
Natasha	a bulldozer. It was a repelling pencil!

Daddy	and do you know the name of the day that comes after Sunday?
Natasha	Saturday
Daddy	No. Saturday comes *before* Sunday. The name of the day that comes *after* Sunday is Monday
Natasha	Monday
Daddy	and the day after that?
Natasha	Tuesday
Daddy	and after that?
Natasha	Wednesday
Daddy	and after that?
Natasha	(*thinks*)
Daddy	Thursday, and after that?
Natasha	Friday
Daddy	and after that?
Natasha	Saturday
Daddy	and what day is this?
Natasha	Monday
Daddy	no it comes before Saturday because Saturday's tomorrow
Natasha	Friday. It's Friday

Later

Natasha	it's going to be my birthday soon
Jutta	that's right, only fourteen days

Ronnie	what date?
Jutta	the twenty-fourth
Natasha	I can't wait till it's my birthday
Ronnie	what's the hurry
Natasha	I can't wait to get all my presents
	I'm going to get more presents than Adam aren't I?
Ronnie	not necessarily. Adam gets presents on his birthday and you get presents on yours. I don't know who will get most
Natasha	but I'll get more presents than Adam on my birthday
Ronnie	Oh yes you don't have to worry about that. When it's Adam's birthday he gets all the presents and you don't get any and on your birthday you'll get all the presents and Adam won't get any
Natasha	but Omilie (*Jutta's mother*) may send him a present
Jutta	that's right. She normally sends something to everyone
Ronnie	well you'll still get *more* than Adam on your birthday

Natasha wants a *toy* walky-talky and a *real* calculating machine for her birthday

Saturday 10 April 1976

Natasha	you're older than Jutta and you're bigger than Jutta
Me	uhuh
Natasha	Jutta can never get older than you (*reassuringly*) but she could get bigger than you
Me	no she cannot get bigger than me
Natasha	she might (*pause*) why not?
Me	because we've both stopped growing

58

Natasha	you've both stopped growing?
Me	yes
Natasha	I haven't stopped growing. I've got a lot of growing to do yet
Me	I know (*pause*)
Natasha	Daddy? How old are you?
Me	forty-eight (*pause*)
Natasha	when will I stop growing?
Me	I don't know maybe some time around eighteen
Natasha	is that how old Jutta is?
Me	no. Jutta's twice as old as eighteen. She's thirty-six
Natasha	eighteen and forty-eight sound the same word
Me	they don't sound *quite* the same word when you're forty-eight (*pause*)
Natasha	there's a man who said Adam and I are younger than we are
Me	Oh really. How could you be younger than you are?
Natasha	I don't know that's just what he said
Me	did you ask him what he meant?
Natasha	no I did not
Me	what was he like?
Natasha	his fingers cracked when he moved them fast like this (*suddenly giving a most convincingly alarming demonstration*) and not when he moved them slowly
Me	and what do you think he meant?
Natasha	I expect he meant what he said
Me	you wouldn't care to put what he meant into any other words?
Natasha	No. I do not care to put it into any other words

Natasha	when's your birthday?
Daddy	in October
Natasha	how long is that?
Daddy	about half a year
Natasha	when is mine?
Daddy	yours is almost a year away
Natasha	is yours before mine then?
Daddy	yes
Natasha	will it always be before mine?
Daddy	no after I have my birthday, your birthday will be before mine

Breakfast

Daddy	Natasha you don't need all that muesli
Natasha	yes I do
Daddy	you're only taking all that amount because Adam took that amount
Natasha	I'm taking *more* than Adam
Daddy	but you're not going to eat all that are you? you should take only what you're going to eat
Natasha	I'm going to *eat more* than Adam
Daddy	but it's just what *you* want to eat it isn't a question of how much *Adam* eats
Natasha	yes it is

Monday   **3 May 1976**

At dinner

Daddy	Adam. I heard you say to Natasha
Adam	Oh I know I know
Daddy	you said to Natasha
Adam	when?

Daddy	at breakfast on Saturday morning
Adam	Oh I know I know I was just joking
Daddy	you said
Adam	I didn't
Daddy	you said to Natasha that if she swore to God and broke her word God would hate her
Adam	no I didn't. I said if she made a promise to God and didn't keep it, it's a sin
Daddy	I heard you say
Adam	that was just joking. I never said anything like that
Jutta	he's a real wriggler. He'll try to wriggle his way out of anything
Adam	I was just joking
Daddy	just joking about that sort of thing is a sin
Adam	I never said anything like that
Daddy	well don't ever again

May 1976

Natasha	daddy would you undo my button, because when I undo it, it ends up being done up

Wednesday 12 May 1976

Last night

Adam	Can I have three pounds for the school?
Daddy	what for?
Adam	I'm making a radio set with Frank, and we need some parts
Daddy	Oh
Adam	yes. Frank's paid for them out of his money
Daddy	Oh well I suppose so – who's Frank anyway?

Adam	Frank knows all sorts of things – about science, birds; he knows the names of all the birds, and stars and astronomy. You would really like to talk to Frank; and he knows about trees and . . .
Daddy	uh hu but *what* is Frank then?
Adam	Frank's the headmaster of the secondary school
Daddy	Oh really! Frank. He's the Headmaster. Frank. what's he like?
Adam	he sometimes gets angry
Daddy	Oh does he? what happens then?
Adam	he starts to shout. He shouts
Daddy	what?
Adam	he shouts 'stop it!'
Daddy	stop what?
Adam	Oh he doesn't like us carrying on making a lot of noise – messing things up – breaking things. You would like to talk to him about science, about the stars, and about the galaxies, and nebulae, and about trees, and birds.

Thursday   **13 May 1976**

Natasha	daddy?
Daddy	yes Natasha
Natasha	do people tell the truth on television?
Daddy	sometimes they do and sometimes they don't
Natasha	when do they tell the truth?
Daddy	there is no way of knowing that for sure
Natasha	do they tell the truth when it's *The News*?
Daddy	sometimes they do and sometimes they don't
Natasha	sometimes they tell lies and sometimes they just tell the truth?
Daddy	yep

Natasha	daddy?
Daddy	uh uh?
Natasha	when's your birthday?
Daddy	my birthday's in October
Natasha	is it tomorrow?
Daddy	Oh no, October is a lot of tomorrows away (*pause*) why do you think it's tomorrow?
Natasha	because you've been waiting so long
Daddy	but you wait just as long
Natasha	no I don't
Daddy	everyone waits the same number of sleeps, or days between birthdays (*pause*) Do you think some people wait longer than others?
Natasha	yes

May 1976

Max is crying. Jutta is out. I want to work

Daddy	Natasha! Will you take Max for half an hour

There is no reply

Daddy	Natasha!

No reply

Daddy	Natasha, if you take Max for half an hour I'll give you five pence
Natasha	alright

She takes Max. After ten minutes

Natasha	how many minutes now?
Daddy	ten minutes
Natasha	but ten minutes is more than half an hour
Daddy	no it isn't

63

	She swings Max up and down, up and down and with every down swing
Natasha	all the way down to God
Daddy	what did you say?
Natasha	nothing
Daddy	all the way *down* to God?
Natasha	yes (*laughing*)
Daddy	how do you mean?
Natasha	I was talking to Max
Daddy	well say it again so I know what you mean
Natasha	I don't want to say it again 'cos I've forgotten it already

Sunday **16 May 1976**

Natasha	mummy. Does God know everything?
Mummy	I don't know
Natasha	do fairies go up to God?
Mummy	I don't know
Natasha	Adam says they do (*pause*) but they can come down again and see their mummies, and they can go to church, and sing to God; and then they go to their homes underground

Thursday **20 May 1976**

Dinner

Pussycat jumps on the table and sniffs at the cheese

64

Daddy	pussycat!
Mummy	yes pussycat! take him off. He may have something
Natasha	what?
Mummy	some germs that are bad for us
Natasha	you've just made me unhungry
Daddy	how?
Natasha	the soup's changed its taste
Daddy	the soup's the same though it tastes different to you
Natasha	no it isn't, the soup's changed
Daddy	mummy's soup hasn't changed
Natasha	yes it has
Daddy	mine's the same
Natasha	well mine's different. I don't want it now
Daddy	the soup's the same. Mummy's remark about the cat made a difference to you but not to the soup
Natasha	well how does that make the *soup* taste different?

June 1976

Natasha	if everyone always has their birthday on the same date, how does anyone get older than anyone else?
Daddy	no one ever gets older than anyone else
Natasha	Oh!
Daddy	and no one ever gets younger than anyone else
Natasha	Oh!
	(*pause*)
Daddy	No one gets older than anyone else *because* everyone always has their birthday on the same date
Natasha	Oh
	She still hasn't 'got' it

7 June 1976

Adam is ringing our new front door bell, which chimes, for fun.

I hear myself shouting

> Stop that. Don't do that again unless I
> know it isn't you

Wednesday 9 June 1976

Slowly

Natasha	Monday Tuesday Wednesday Friday Saturday
Jutta	No. Monday Tuesday Wednesday *Thursday* Friday Saturday *Sunday*
Natasha	Monday Tuesday Wednesday Friday Saturday Sunday
Jutta	No. Monday Tuesday Wednesday *Thursday* Friday Saturday Sunday
Natasha	Monday Tuesday Wednesday Thursday Saturday Friday Sunday
Jutta	No. Monday Tuesday Wednesday Thursday *Friday Saturday* Sunday
Natasha	Sunday Monday Tuesday Wednesday Friday Saturday Sunday
Jutta	No. Sunday Monday Tuesday Wednesday Thursday Friday *Saturday*
Natasha	Sunday Tuesday Wednesday Friday Saturday Saturday Sunday
Jutta	No! Sunday *Monday* Tuesday Wednesday *Thursday* Friday Saturday
Ronnie	Natasha
Natasha	yes
Ronnie	Natasha

Presto e poco a poco accel. a prestissimo

Monday Tuesday Wednesday Thursday Friday
Saturday Sunday

66

Natasha	Monday Tuesday Wednesday
Ronnie	Thursday Friday Saturday Sunday
Natasha	Thursday Friday Saturday Sunday
Ronnie	Wednesday Thursday Friday
Natasha	Wednesday Friday Thursday
Ronnie	Wednesday Thursday Friday
Natasha	Wednesday Thursday Friday
Ronnie	Wednesday Thursday Friday
Natasha	Wednesday Thursday Friday
Ronnie	Sunday Monday Tuesday
Natasha	Sunday Monday Tuesday
Ronnie	Wednesday Thursday Friday
Natasha	Wednesday Thursday Friday
Ronnie	Wednesday Thursday Friday Saturday
Natasha	Wednesday Thursday Friday Saturday
Ronnie	Thursday Friday Saturday Sunday
Natasha	Thursday Friday Saturday Sunday
Ronnie	Sunday Monday Tuesday Wednesday Thursday Friday Saturday
Natasha	Sunday Monday Tuesday Wednesday Thursday Friday Saturday
Ronnie	Monday Tuesday Wednesday Thursday Friday Saturday Sunday
Natasha	Monday Tuesday Wednesday Thursday Friday Saturday Sunday
Ronnie	Monday Tuesday Wednesday Thursday Friday Saturday Sunday
Natasha	Monday Tuesday Wednesday Friday Sunday Saturday
Ronnie	you missed out Thursday and you reversed Saturday and Sunday
	Natasha doubles up falls off her chair rolls over on the floor gurgling, splurtling then climbs back
Ronnie	Sunday Monday Tuesday Wednesday Thursday Friday Saturday
Natasha	Monday Tuesday Friday Sunday

Ronnie	you missed out Sunday at the beginning. Wednesday and Thursday in the middle, replaced Saturday by Sunday at the end
	Natasha again 'creases' up into helpless gurgles and splurtles, falls on the floor rolls over and over and clambers up again for more
Ronnie	Monday Tuesday Wednesday Thursday Friday Saturday Sunday
Natasha	Monday Tuesday Wednesday Thursday Saturday Friday Sunday Monday
Ronnie	you reversed Friday and Saturday and put in Monday
	Repeat performance
Natasha	more daddy, more
Daddy	that *tickles* you, doesn't it? it tickles the back of your brain
Natasha	yes (*gurgling and chorkling*) yes daddy, it does. Tickle me daddy So I did

16 June 1976

	Last night
Natasha	where does the snow dance?
Daddy	I don't know
Natasha	at the snow ball

Sunday   **19 June 1976**

Natasha	Daddy, I've played the piano all the way down
	She had started at what we call the bottom left and played her way to the top right

Sunday	**27 June 1976**

Natasha is reading in silence

| Natasha | can you hear me read? |
| Jutta | no, Natasha |

June 1976

| Natasha | Can God kill himself? |
| Mummy | I don't know |

Sunday	**28 June 1976**

Monty is an old friend of mine. Natasha hasn't met him before

Natasha	who gets up in the morning and goes to the shop?
Monty	I don't know
Natasha	the shopkeeper

I told Monty that Jutta had told me, that Natasha had asked her 'Can God kill himself?'

Monty	there is an incredibly close relationship between sex and death. I will tell you what the question is saying. She is asking 'Does God masturbate?'
Ronnie	and that is 'Does Daddy masturbate?'
Monty	precisely. She wishes to know whether you do it without mummy, whether you need mummy: whether she can do it with you instead of mummy
Ronnie	there you go
Monty	I hope you don't mind me being so direct
Ronnie	Oh not at all

A few days ago

Adam	have you heard this one?
Daddy	which one?
Adam	this one
Daddy	which one?
Adam	*this one*
Daddy	aw come on
Adam	well there was this man see
Daddy	yes
Adam	now don't interrupt and when he was a boy his father asked him what he wanted and he asked his father to give him a brain so his father gave him a television set and then he grew up a bit and he became a teenager and his father asked him what he wanted and he asked his father to give him a brain so his father gave him a house then he grew up and became a man and his father again asked him what he wanted and he cried 'Father! will you give me a brain!' so his father gave him a car and he was driving the car and had an accident, lost most of his brains with brain damage and he was in the ambulance being taken to hospital, with his brain damage you see, and his father was sitting beside him and he said to his father: 'Father you should have given me a brain.'
Daddy	I don't know whether I think that's funny or not
Natasha	I think it's funny
Daddy	Oh well then

Thursday	8 July 1976

One of Adam's friends stayed the night last night.

Adam	kiss David good night, mummy
David	(*aged eight*) Oh I'm sorry I only allow myself to be kissed by my mummy and other relatives

Monday	28 July 1976

Adam	have you been to the *core* of the earth?
Daddy	no
Adam	why not? no one's been there. it's very hot and very deep
Natasha	deeper than this table

Adam	they said on TV that the Xmas holiday was going to be longer this year
Daddy	yes
Adam	how can it be longer? does it mean it's going to be longer *till* Xmas?
Daddy	they can make the Xmas holiday longer, but they can't make it longer *till* Xmas

July 1976

Daddy	have you seen a box of matches
Natasha	yes there's one on the dresser

I went to the dresser. Natasha went with me. I wondered why. I found the box of matches, took one out, struck it, and lit a cigarette. She was watching me all the time

71

Natasha	(*nonplussed*) but Adam said they're the pretend matches
Daddy	well this one's lit
Natasha	can I have a go?

She takes the box, takes a match out of it, strikes it. It lights

Natasha	but these are the *pretend* matches
Daddy	that's what Adam said
Natasha	but they *are* the pretend matches
Daddy	Adam must have made a mistake
Natasha	but I put them there
Daddy	well?
Natasha	can I try another
Daddy	No. They're not very many. I don't want them all used up
Natasha	Oh can I try another
Daddy	well, ok

she tries another. It lit also

Natasha	some are pretend matches and some are real
Daddy	I bet you they're all real
Natasha	I put them *exactly* there
Daddy	Adam must have changed the matches
Natasha	No. No one could have changed them. (*pause*) Oh Daddy! (*in extreme vexation*). (*pause*). The matches must have changed

August 1976

Natasha	and what is 'swearing'?
Ronnie	some words refer to God and Divine things. If they are used trivially, or mixed up with nasty words, that's swearing
Natasha	what does 'refer to' mean?
Ronnie	the word table refers to an actual table

Natasha	oh yes (*impatiently*)
	and what does 'trivial' mean
Ronnie	unimportant
Natasha	daddy?
Ronnie	yes
Natasha	daddy, what's the opposite of near?
Ronnie	far
Natasha	and what's the opposite of queen?
Ronnie	king
Natasha	and what's the opposite of heaven?
Ronnie	hell
Natasha	and say them one after the other
Ronnie	how do you mean?
Natasha	say the opposite of near
Ronnie	far
Natasha	and the opposite of
Ronnie	yes, ok. far king hell
Natasha	you swore daddy
Ronnie	yes
Natasha	you said farking hell daddy! you swore daddy!

August 1976

Natasha to Paul, her grown-up half-brother

Could you make your mummy laugh when you were a child?

Adam	why did the skeleton not jump over the cliff?
Me	I don't know
Adam	'cos he didn't have any guts

Corfu*	2 September 1976

	The wind is moving the clouds and shaking the branches
Natasha	is the moon shaking

	Nina is younger than Adam and spells very well
Nina	can you spell well?
Adam	I can spell better than you and you can even spell better than me

September 1976

Natasha	what's the first thing you put in a garden?
Arthur	I don't know
Natasha	your foot

Natasha	I don't want to sleep in my bed tonight
Arthur	that's alright with me. You can sleep anywhere as far as I'm concerned
Natasha	I'm going to sleep with you then
Kira	so am I
Nina	so am I
Arthur	(*laughing*) you can't do that
Natasha	why not? Janette sleeps with you so why can't I sleep with you or Kira sleep with you or Nina sleep with you
Arthur	(*laughing*) I'm just sleeping with Janette
Natasha	that's not fair Arthur, that's not fair

*We spent the month of September '76, in Corfu, living together with friends Arthur and Janet, and their children, Kira (aged 8) and Nina (aged 7).

Ronnie	Anyway. Where do you *want* to sleep?
Natasha	I want to sleep in his nostril
Nina	I want to sleep in his ear
Kira	I want to sleep inside daddy's penis

5 September 1976

Natasha is holding up a little wheel

have you seen Max's invisible car?

| Everyone | no |
| Natasha | its got invisible doors, invisible seats, an invisible engine, and three invisible wheels. It's – *invisible*! |

September 1976

Fish for lunch

Adam	(*to me*) supposing you were very very very hungry, you had no food, and you were going to die of starvation, would you eat your wife?
Ronnie	you mean Jutta?
Adam	yes
Ronnie	not if she were alive. If she were completely dead, and I would die if there was nothing to eat, I might eat her body. I might, I might
Arthur	who knows who we're eating now?
Ronnie	would you eat mummy?
Adam	no I wouldn't eat mummy
Jutta	would you eat Max?
Ronnie	would you eat me?
Arthur	do you know that Buddhist story? a couple come to a desert with their son. There is nothing to eat. They are starving. They have to cross the desert. The father offers himself to be eaten, and

	the wife. But they decide that the pair of them without a child have a chance, but one of them with a child has no chance. They can always have another child. So they eat their son. And the Buddhists say that anything we eat we should eat as though it's one's own child
Ronnie	or one's grannie. This fish could be my grannie
Janette	do you recognize her by the smell?
Ronnie	my grannie always dreamed of swimming in the Mediterranean, so she reincarnated as a fish and was happy just swimming around as she had always dreamed of when she was caught and now we're eating her
Adam	(*credulously*) did your grannie
Ronnie	(*interrupting*) No I just made it up
Jutta	this conversation is putting me off my food
Arthur	you're the only one it seems to have taken this way

10 September 1976

Adam	why don't you write a book on swearing?
Ronnie	a book on swearing?
Adam	yes. Write a book on what swearing *means*. You know, fuckin' hell, and fuckin' this and fuckin' that and expressions like that. Write a book and tell people what that sort of thing *means*

Corfu   September 1976

	For days, not a cloud in the sky. Just that Mediterranean sun
Adam	Do you think the sun is having his revenge on the clouds?

10 September 1976

A few of Adam's questions today, his ninth
birthday.

How is the timing of a hand–grenade regulated?
Does lead sink in mercury?
Why does even a grain of sand sink in water?
Why does even one drop of water fall through
the air?
and,
Why does a bazooka tremble?

Saturday   **11 September 1976**

Adam eats breakfast as much standing or jumping
up and down as sitting. How many times has he
been told to say please and thank you and pass
back what has been passed to him and to look
where the honey or the jam or the butter is
before calling out for it.
and

Arthur	look at me when you ask for something Adam
	and
Jutta	eat with your mouth empty
Adam	eat with my mouth empty!
Ronnie	he got you this time
Adam	ho ho ho
Ronnie	anyway it's obvious what she meant
Adam	speak with your mouth shut

Natasha	Ronnie, I mean, Daddy
Daddy	yes Natasha
Natasha	how many years till my birthday?
Daddy	but Natasha, I've told you, from one birthday to the next is one year, so it's always less than a year till your next birthday

Natasha tells me that she's never had a nightmare

September 1976

In a dispute over a toy

Natasha he gave it to me
Adam *he* gave it to *you* and
    I gave it to *me*

September 1976

After dinner. The stars are out. We're all off to
make a fire on the beach. Arthur leading the
way.

Natasha Daddy!? Will you give me a carry?
Daddy Yes, Natasha

And I hoist her up on my shoulders. For how
long shall I still be able to do that?

Natasha but don't crackle my toes
Daddy alright Natasha
Natasha Arthur's crackled them already

Ah! Now I'm no longer the only one who is
allowed to crackle her toes

Night

we are lying on our backs surveying the stars

Daddy how did all this come about?
Adam do you mean 'who made it?'?
Daddy well not exactly, but alright
Adam a dead man
Daddy a dead man?! how do you mean?
Adam yes. A dead human being

At breakfast

Daddy	what did you mean by a dead human being? A ghost?
Adam	a ghost, a spirit
Daddy	a spirit
Adam	yes when you die. One spirit goes up (*indicating from the top of his head*) and another goes down – the good one goes up and the bad one goes down
Daddy	and they are both in us while we are alive?
Adam	yes
Daddy	and how do you mean a spirit made all this?
Adam	no I don't really mean a spirit made all *this*
Daddy	the stars?
Adam	the stars were there before we were. some people say God made it. God's a spirit. But I don't think God made it. Do you think God exists Arthur?
Arthur	yes I think God exists
Adam	God must have been born
Daddy	how could God be born? If he exists, he must be always, forever
Adam	how did God walk on the earth then? and anyway who made God?
Kira	(*to Arthur*) mummy and you made me
Arthur	we didn't *make* you
Kira	where did I come from then?
Nina	people come from people. And God made the first people
Adam	People come from creatures who were like monkeys. They had smaller brains. And they came from other creatures. Before they were them there were dinosaurs and things like that, and fishes and the sea. This planet is like the stars. It comes from gases. And then things

79

began to grow and some grew into people. And they developed science and technology, from iron and metals, and made things like we have now, knives and razor blades, and telephones and typewriters, and cars and aeroplanes and telescopes and things like that – they developed science and technology, that's how we find out things, by science

Wednesday 15 September 1976

During supper

Adam	Come on, come on
Daddy	how do you mean 'Come on, come on'?
Adam	Come on, Come on. Swear! Swear! Let me hear you swearing.
Daddy	come on, come on yourself. I don't feel like swearing. Why do you want to hear me swearing?
Adam	I want you to swear
Daddy	I don't want to swear
Adam	swear! go on swear!
Daddy	I don't feel like swearing
Adam	swear!
Daddy	why?
Adam	I want to join you
Daddy	you want to join me?
Adam	yes I want to join you
Daddy	why do you want to join me?
Adam	in order to get you out of it
Daddy	in order to get me out of it?
Adam	yes, in order to get you out of it (*pause*)
Daddy	that's one reason I started it
Adam	Oh
Daddy	Oh yes. That was one reason. I joined them in

	order to get them out of it. And then I got into the habit myself
Adam	oh
	(*pause*)
Daddy	but I don't feel like it anymore
Adam	Oh no?
Daddy	no
Adam	no?
Daddy	is that alright then?
Adam	that's alright then
Daddy	ok?
Adam	ok

Corfu   September 1976

Afternoon on the beach.

Adam sights an unidentified object floating fairly far out to sea. He proposes a 'project' with 'component operations'. Basically, he, Arthur and I are to swim out to it, identify it, and if 'feasible', bring it ashore.

The first 'component operation' passed uneventfully. Arthur, he and I stand on an off-shore rock. Each throws his goggles and snorkel into the sea, dives in after them, retrieves them, puts them on.

Operation Two is to swim out to unidentified floating object. We set off together. Soon Adam and Arthur were drawing ahead of me, and it was not long before I had swam further out than I had done for at least twenty-five years. Further was too far. The object, a black shape, looked just as far away as it had done from the shore. Adam and Arthur seemed thirty or forty feet further out. Then Arthur stopped. Adam was still for going on, but Arthur ordered him back. They swam back together to where I was and the three of us swam back to shore together.

I was grateful to feel the sand under my wobbling knees and very glad to sink back into the safe sand.

Arthur looked quite relieved. Adam was livid. I've never seen
him so enraged. He was *hopping* mad. He threw himself on
the sand, and squirmed and twitched around like an eel with
frustration.

He blamed it all on Arthur, for turning back.

Arthur	Don't blame me! It was *way* off
Adam	No it wasn't

Jutta had been watching from the shore

Jutta	You were only half-way there
Adam	No we weren't. We were almost there
Daddy	No we were not almost there. It was still *far* away. Definitely *too* far away
Adam	it wasn't
Daddy	It was
Arthur	Adam! (he wasn't listening) Adam!! Your mummy saw it from the shore
Adam	she did not
Daddy	It was too far

Adam looked at us all

Daddy	I'm telling you. It was too far
Arthur	It was still far away
Jutta	You weren't even half way there

He was completely surrounded

Adam	You're all lying
Arthur	Look. Why should we lie to you Adam. We're all friends

Adam said nothing

Arthur	It was too far for me, and it was definitely too far for you

He still said nothing

Daddy	Look. You still can't swim further than Arthur, or me, even
Adam	How do you know

Daddy	Your mummy saw us from the shore
	We were only half way there
Jutta	that's right
Adam	she's lying
Jutta	No I'm not. You won't listen to anyone that's your trouble
Adam	well I'm not going to listen to you
Jutta	You'd better watch it. You had better watch it
Daddy	Do you seriously think that you know better than everyone else

Adam said nothing
We all took a short breather. Except Adam, who was still 'at it', though he was silent

Daddy	Anyway. It's not a defeat
Adam	Yes it is

And it all started up again. After the third full round of the above, with minor variations, Adam's vehemence had in no way abated

Jutta	it was an optical illusion
Adam	a what?
Jutta	an optical illusion
Adam	An optical illusion!? What is an 'optical illusion'?
Jutta	something that looks different from what it is
Adam	you mean I can't believe my eyes?!
Daddy	Well. Not always. Not just like that. Not without reservations
Adam	reservations!?

It went on and on

Evening

Adam	if you had a wish what would it be?
Me	can it be for a state or a thing or
Adam	anything you like
Me	I would like to be happy – if I was *happy* then a lot of things would have to be right
Adam	and what would your next wish be?
Me	that everyone else be happy
Adam	*everyone*? in the whole world?
Me	yes. why not?
Adam	even against their will?
Jutta	do you think there's anyone who doesn't want to be happy?
Me	well ok. I don't want to *force* anyone to be happy. Let's say all those who want to be happy can be happy (*pause*)
Adam	daddy?
Daddy	yes
Adam	would you rather be strong or weak?
Daddy	I would rather be strong
Adam	would you rather be wise or stupid?
Daddy	I would rather be wise
Adam	would you rather be weak and wise, or stupid and strong?
Daddy	weak and wise
Adam	and would you rather be happy and weak, or proud and strong
Daddy	happy and weak

October 1976

Natasha	Did you write this book?*
Daddy	yes
Natasha	they've printed it very well (*turning the pages*) there's not much on the paper. Look, there's hardly anything on that page. Or that page. There's the littlest *I've* ever seen. I think this is the *silliest* book I've ever seen

28 October 1976

Adam	daddy?
Daddy	yes Adam
Adam	when's my birthday?
Daddy	don't you know your birthday by now?
Adam	yes but how long is it till my birthday?
Daddy	how do you mean?
Adam	how many months?
Daddy	don't you know the months of the year yet?
Adam	Oh come on daddy
Daddy	well this is October. Then it'll be November, December, January, February, March, April, May, June, July, August, *September*
Adam	Oh my God
Daddy	well there's no hurry
Jutta	everyone's got a birthday before you except daddy
Adam	Oh (*petulantly*)
Daddy	don't you know that yet? anyway I'm in no hurry for my next birthday
Adam	*I'm* in a hurry
Daddy	you'll never be nine again
Adam	I don't want to be
Daddy	Your next birthday you'll be ten
Adam	I know. I can't wait

*Do You Love Me?

85

Daddy	you should make the most of every day in your life
	Every minute
	you'll never have a second over again
Adam	would you like to be young again?
	would you like to be nine again?
	would you like to be eighteen again?
	come on answer. would you like to be twenty-eight again?
Daddy	would I like my life over again?

November 1976

| Adam | daddy, will you teach me a Christmas carol, in a *smart* key |

Thursday   30 December 1976

Night

Jutta, Adam, Natasha, and Max have just returned from Stuttgart after a week with Opa and Omilie, and the rest of Jutta's family.
I came back home a few days earlier.
Now, Natasha and I are sitting snugly on the sofa, snow and frost outside.

Natasha	were you playing the piano when we rang the bell?
Daddy	no
Natasha	were you watching television?
Daddy	no
Natasha	were you having something to eat?
Daddy	no
Natasha	were you writing?
Daddy	no
Natasha	were you walking up and down?
Daddy	no

Natasha	were you smoking your pipe?
Daddy	no
Natasha	were you studying?
Daddy	no
Natasha	were you just sitting down?!
Daddy	I was just sitting down
Natasha	Oh, at last I know what you were doing when we rang the bell
Daddy	And I was waiting for you to ring the bell
Natasha	did you know we were coming?
Daddy	I was expecting you
Natasha	but did you *know* we were coming?
Daddy	well when I got back from Stuttgart it was just twenty past seven, so I was looking at my watch and it was just twenty past seven so I thought I would just sit down and wait for the doorbell to ring
Natasha	and did you know it was going to ring
Daddy	I thought it would then I heard your voices, and then I knew it would, and it did. Just at twenty-five minutes past seven

A hug

January 1977

Evening in my study

Natasha	(*comes in: offers me some bubble gum*) I can blow a bubble with this bubble gum (*pause*) (*reluctantly*) I did it for the first time this afternoon (*she is not getting on very well at it now*) Can you blow bubble gum?
Daddy	(*has a go: unsuccessful*) no
Natasha	yes you can. Adam can blow *big* ones.
Daddy	well there you are that's something he can do I can't do
Natasha	you can't blow bubble gum! (*incredulously*)

87

Daddy	when I was your age I wasn't allowed bubble gum so I never got the practice (*evidently this is not a sufficient excuse*) and when I grew up I never felt in the mood
Natasha	and you're the oldest, and you can't blow bubble gum!
Daddy	well maybe I *could* if I tried, but I've never put my mind to it
Natasha	(*wandering off, shaking her head*) and you're the oldest and you can't blow bubble gum

---

Jutta, Adam, Natasha, and I saw the New Year in together, over a bottle of champagne
Adam became engrossed with how the cork could have been gotten into the bottle

>   'Keep that cork, I want to study it'

February 1977

Natasha has been playing a Haydn Air and a melody, on the piano.

She had the idea of playing them together

I told her she had discovered counterpoint!
But she wasn't interested

28 February 1977

It's the end of another late night Western

The goodie and the baddie stand facing each
other for what can only be the last time

They draw
The badman begins to fall
His eyes turn up. He has a final glimpse of the
sun

Natasha   He said 'Do You Love Me?'

He dies

March 1977

Jutta is taken aback by coming upon Adam
making grandiose magical passes with a stick at
our ailing palm tree in the hall

Jutta   Can I believe my eyes?
Can I believe my eyes?

Adam   No

Later

Jutta   I couldn't believe my ears